DEEPER INTO THE MESS
Praying Through Tough Times

BRENDAN McMANUS SJ & JIM DEEDS

Published by Messenger Publications, 2019

ISBN 978 1 78812 021 0

Designed by Messenger Publications Design Department
Typeset in Candara and Blog Script
Photographs by the authors except page 24 © Jozef Klopacka / Shutterstock
Printed by Hussar Books

Messenger Publications,
37 Lower Leeson Street, Dublin D02 W938
www.messenger.ie

CONTENTS

Introduction

People love to talk, to relate to others. In fact, we are built for communicating; our speech, faces, gestures, hands and bodies are all means of relating to others – think of how a hug can communicate much more effectively than words. Even more basically, we are built for communication with God, our creator and origin. Relating to God should be easy as it is an essential part of who we are. However, it can get very complicated as we can feel God is too distant, or that we are not smart enough. We can even doubt that God would be interested in us. When we hit difficult moments, God seems to have abandoned us and prayer can seem impossible.

However, given that we are created in the image of God, it is possible to live our lives close to God in a personal and intimate way. 'God is closer to us than we are to ourselves' said St Augustine. This is a miracle. God is always with us, close and intimate, but often we are not with God. How could we miss out on something so immediate and essential? Why do people find it so hard, or feel that it is useless or give up on it entirely? People often end up concluding that there is no God, or if their God is distant and doesn't care that God's not there for them when they need help. We've often had experiences of being let down, feeling alone or really struggling in prayer. Sometimes we can overcomplicate things, feeling we have to **do** a lot in prayer, that we need a lot of things (special place, books, knowledge), perhaps suspecting that God has a negative view of us and that we don't measure up. To relate to God the way you would to a close friend seems to be taking liberties, a bit too simple or too close for comfort. Yet how are we to relate to God except in the ways in which we are designed to do so: using words, gestures, symbols and our bodies? Think of how powerful it is to appeal to God in heartfelt words, kneeling or holding our hands open, and repeating the words of a prayer such as 'Lord Jesus, have mercy on me, a sinner'.

One of the great things about a 'close' God is that it doesn't really matter how you pray as long as you find a way of communicating;

God will meet us more than halfway. In any close, loving relationship, people find a way, despite difficulties, to relate through words, gestures, signs or symbols. Think of Mary at the foot of the Cross, just standing there wordless; sometimes being there is enough. It is about finding some way that works; each of us is different and different things will work for us. As Pope Francis says, each of us has our own path to God, given that we are uniquely made (*Gaudete et Exsultate* 11). Some of us use sight, some actions, some words, some gestures to communicate our love for others. Our job is to try out different ways of praying and learn what works in terms of God becoming more and more the centre of our lives.

St Ignatius said that God deals directly with us and is **always trying to reach us**, so our job is to recognise where God is present in our everyday lives. Even in the mess of things, in the dirt and muck of things, God is always there. That may be unexpected but it is liberating. Our job is to spot where God is calling and learn to respond, helping us to transform the situations where we find ourselves. There is no point in making the same old prayers in the same old way if God is waiting for a creative response and looking to make something new of us. This is an adventure into the unknown where we can take some pointers from wise people who have gone before us, but it is also one where we have to trust our instincts and believe that God is offering us new opportunities. Make your prayers real, heartfelt and based on your experience, and step out into the unknown. God is waiting.

Accordingly, the meditations in this book are divided into five chapters or groupings that roughly follow the dynamic of St Ignatius's Spiritual Exercises:

- We are created by God;
- God deals directly with us;
- When darkness is all around (God appears absent);
- Being with Christ on the Cross;
- God turns everything to the good.

Each is preceded by a short 'Conversation with God' that models how we might relate to God directly, praying with every aspect of our lives and bringing God's light into the darkest corners.

Some Ways of Praying

While this is not a book on prayer methods, nor does it cover important areas such as liturgical prayer, devotional prayer, adoration etc., it does attempt to present a way of praying in particularly difficult situations: emergency prayer, if you like, that can be useful when other methods don't work. It is based on the approach of St Ignatius and tested in the experience of the authors. Each of the main meditations that follows is divided into four sections:

1. INTRODUCTION OR DESCRIPTION OF THE SITUATION
   The human experience while often one of joy or happiness can also involve suffering, abandonment or loneliness. These experiences are common to us all, but when you are in the middle of them, it feels like you are the only one. It can be easy to forget that others have been through these more testing situations have prayed and survived, and that God is with us all in the middle of this. This first step is acknowledging the reality of the situation, which can be overpowering and frightening sometimes, and accepting that God is with us in this.

2. THE WAY OF PRAYING FOR THAT SITUATION
   This means handing the situation over to God, acknowledging that it is often beyond us and that we need help. There is a real humility in this that acknowledges our own neediness and is a heartfelt appeal to the one who made us. This is where the communication happens and, as in most situations, it takes some adjustment and experimentation to find the best way of expressing oneself.

3. RELEVANT SCRIPTURE TEXTS
   Scripture is made up of stories of biblical characters who found a way to relate to God, found rituals and words that made up their prayer. Even Moses, David and Job have ongoing conversations with God – things change and their prayer has to change to keep

up with where God is leading them. It's always challenging but ultimately worthwhile; think about the journey the biblical characters have to go on to be open to God – as always, Mary is the best example. Obviously, Jesus himself as recorded in the Gospels has a special place in this prayer.

4. A SUGGESTED RITUAL OR ACTION TO EMBODY THE PRAYER

As we are body and spirit, we need to express our feelings externally in some concrete way. This means finding an action, ritual or physical expression that supports the prayer: think of the power of pilgrimage. When we pray with our whole being it makes the prayer much more powerful.

In some ways this can be a journey into the unknown, trusting that the Spirit works within us and that we will be guided towards peace and healing. There are no shortcuts here, however, and this can be challenging and painful as we pass through the experience of the Cross. Being with Christ is an adventure in which we are sometimes not sure of the destination but we place our trust in our guide.

It is an invitation to build on the wisdom of the past, but also to make it our own, personalising it in order that we might follow God more closely and give ourselves to him. God is not trapped in the past, in books or institutions, but is a living presence in the experience of our lives now.

Sacred Space

You may find it easier to pray if you make a sacred space in your home, preferably a quiet place where you can be undisturbed. You may already have a shelf with a candle, Bible or a holy picture. This might be a good place. Otherwise, you could create a new space for objects, icons or photos that draw you to prayer as you read the book. Even if you don't have a physical place you can create one mentally, using your imagination to picture a place, a face or a memory of being loved.

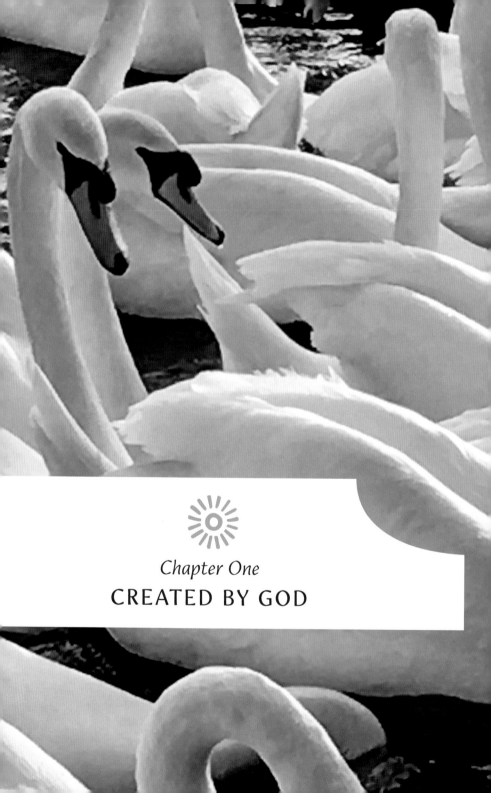

Chapter One

CREATED BY GOD

God freely created us so that we might know,
love, and serve God in this life and be happy with God forever.
Ignatius Loyola, *Spiritual Exercises* #23

CONVERSATION WITH GOD
Speaking as one friend to another

Me: Hello ... God?

God: Hello my friend. A new day starts.

Me: I just wanted to say thank you for this brand new day.

*God: I am making this day just as I have made you. Rejoice in that fact
and accept the day to come.*

*Me: I will. Today when I got up and looked at the sky, I got the feeling it
would be a day of possibilities.*

God: I like that! Tell me more.

*Me: I had a sense that, today, well ... that something new is possible!
What has happened has happened. What is to come hasn't
happened yet.*

*God: I Am all possibility. Today I create all things anew. Old hurts can
heal. Today new challenges can be faced. Today the lost and lonely
can be consoled. Today the hungry can eat. Today and all days,
you, my friend, can play your part.*

*Me: I see my challenge. I see my responsibilities. But in this moment I
feel alive and close to you.*

*God: I am in all ways close to you. The moments when you allow yourself
to feel that closeness are, indeed, moments of possibility. Use this
day wisely.*

Me: I will look for your way and walk close to you.

God: And I will light the way. Go ...

It's good to talk.

The Glory of Our Being

This rather wonderful thing is a piece of bark from an old tree that stands tall in the Falls Park in Belfast.

On the outside the bark was pretty rough looking. It was weathered and gnarly and a bit dull.

However, as you can see here, on the inside it has smoothness and colours that are at once subtle as well as striking. Who would have thought that the brown bark would have had purple, pink and orange tones inside it? I find it beautiful.

On the outside, the bark appeared bumpy and chaotic, but what is apparent is that on the inside it has a complex shape and structure. It is ordered for its purpose of allowing the tree to grow from its heartland, its core.

Funny thing – having seen its true nature from the inside, we now have a different way of seeing the outside of the bark too. We can't *not* see its true interior nature now. As a result, we see that it's beautiful both inside and out.

Do you know someone who feels a bit like the outside of the bark? Are you that someone yourself? If so, what do we learn from the picture of the inside of the bark? What would we tell that person or even ourselves about the nature of ourselves?

So many fail to see the glory and beauty of their inner being. Many people get caught up in the messiness and imperfection encountered in life and in themselves. That messiness and imperfection can be mistaken for failure, ugliness or even a reason to hate.

When we're in that mode, we fail to see how complex, well ordered and smooth we are at our heart and core. We have been created and are being created daily as well. Not only that, but the One who creates us loves us and wants to be in dialogue with us. It is possible to take our feelings of messiness and imperfection to our Creator and to understand that our Creator is with us even, and maybe especially, in those times.

When we do, it is possible to reconnect to the beauty within, to the purpose of our lives, to the glory of our being.

Meditation

'I am beautiful – inside and out. I am glorious at my core. I have been created and created well. I can love me and love all.'

Scripture

Isaiah 43:1 But now thus says the Lord, he who created you, O Jacob, he who formed you, O Israel: Do not fear, for I have redeemed you; I have called you by name, you are mine.

Ephesians 2:10 For we are what he has made us, created in Christ Jesus for good works, which God prepared beforehand to be our way of life.

Songs of Songs 4:7 You are altogether beautiful, my love; there is no flaw in you.

Action

Go to a park or forest and break off a (small) piece of bark. Look at the inside of the bark and see its beauty. Keep the bark in your sacred or special place.

The Old and the Gnarly

It strikes me that this Cross has a certain sensibility and dignity – beauty even – despite and because of its age and its roughness.

Look at it for a few moments and allow your mind to wander and wonder.

Now sit back and relax for a while. Sit with the image of God as the 'vine' and us as branches. What might this mean?

Because we don't live in a country where grapes are grown we don't really know what a vine looks like. I had images of a smooth green or brown trunk that was very beautiful. How else would Jesus describe God?

But ... a vine is an old gnarled trunk that has aged in the ground over many decades. It lays down firm roots and each year shoots out vibrant, fruit-filled branches. Once the branches have borne their fruit and lived their lives, they are cut away. The vine remains. Most people see the branches and the fruit, not the old, wise vine. And yet the branches would not exist without the vine. Lovely!

The image of the branches also strikes us as meaningful. Each branch is connected to the vine, and they are therefore connected to each other through the vine. Maybe the outer edges of the branches do not contemplate the vine. They may not even know or believe it exists. Being a branch may seem all there is. And yet, the vine is there, knowing, growing and caring for those branches in the same way as it grows the branches closer to the vine and knows of their existence. No hierarchies for the vine. Just branches to grow.

Meditation

Take a few moments to sit with this image of God as an old, wise, deeply rooted vine, pulsing with an energy that God transmits to us – life itself. God wants us to thrive, grow and be fruitful. Stay with this image and see what comes up for you.

🌸 What would you want to say to God the vine?

🌸 What do you hear?

🌸 To whom are you connected and for whom do you want to be grateful?

🌸 Where are the areas of disconnect in your life?

🌸 How might you reconnect, even a little? Think small, practical steps here.

Scripture

John 15:5 I am the vine, you are the branches. Those who abide in me and I in them bear much fruit, because apart from me you can do nothing.

Isaiah 46:4 Even to your old age I am he, even when you turn grey I will carry you. I have made, and I will bear; I will carry and will save.

1 Corinthians 1:25 For God's foolishness is wiser than human wisdom, and God's weakness is stronger than human strength.

Action

Find a small, twisted twig. Bring it home and put it in the sacred space in your home. Notice its twists and turns. Notice its rough edges. Notice its complexity and come to see its beauty.

Bringing Balance to Our Lives

When making an acoustic guitar, two of the factors that the craftsperson considers are how long the notes will sustain or last and how well they will be heard (volume or output or impact).

The strength and rigidity of the body governs how long the note lasts (sustains) and volume or impact is governed by the flexibility of the body. Therefore acoustic guitars are not solid but essentially box-like; they have thinly topped shallow bodies that can make imperceptible movements when the string is struck.

There is an essential wisdom in all of this – the constant challenge to find the **balance** between having sustainability (keeping ourselves strong, safe and well) and output (impacting on the world and those around us) is one that we face daily, both as individuals and as groups of people.

If we focus too much on ourselves and our own sustainability we can become self-obsessed and introspective. We won't let our voices of love, joy and mercy be heard by those who might just need to hear them.

Too much volume and output into the world without taking care of sustainability might mean that we will be prone to burn-out. We might also put people off because our own volume and actions might crowd out the voices or actions of others – we might just miss some of the richness others have to offer.

Meditation

St Ignatius Loyola also used the idea of balance, reminding us that to be free to move the way God wants us to go we have to be light on our feet, not too attached to things, holding them lightly. He says we must hold ourselves at the point of balance, in the healthy tension of being ready but not impulsive.

※ What are my unhelpful attachments or addictions, the things that don't allow me to move freely?

※ What are the signs that I am under- or over-doing things – how can I create a healthy tension or balance in my life?

※ What is God asking of me in my life, in terms of direction and commitments?

※ What direction do I need to go in; where is the real creativity, life and energy for me?

Scripture

Ecclesiastes 3:1–8 For everything there is a season, and a time for every matter under heaven: a time to be born, and a time to die; a time to plant, and a time to pluck up what is planted; a time to kill, and a time to heal; a time to break down, and a time to build up; a time to weep, and a time to laugh; a time to mourn, and a time to dance.

1 Corinthians 13:1 If I speak in the tongues of mortals and of angels, but do not have love, I am a noisy gong or a clanging cymbal.

Philippians 4:8 Finally, beloved, whatever is true, whatever is honourable, whatever is just, whatever is pure, whatever is pleasing, whatever is commendable, if there is any excellence and if there is anything worthy of praise, think about these things.

Action

Get two tennis balls (or even two stones) and hold one in each hand. Look at them and see how holding them in this way is balanced and easy.

Now put or try to put both in one hand while holding out the other empty hand. Experience how difficult this is to do and how out of balance it feels when there is too much in one hand and not enough in the other.

Now go back to holding one tennis ball in each hand and feel how the balance is restored. Pray in this position for a little while. Ask God to help you restore balance in those areas of your life where it has been lost.

Transforming Failure

Few things in life are certain, but one of the certainties of life is this: we will make mistakes. We will make a lot of mistakes. Early in life we often feel guilty and ashamed of our mistakes, perhaps thinking that we are the only ones who make them. As we grow older, however, we see that making mistakes – messing things up and failure – is part of life for everyone. While mistakes are not to be sought out, they are not the end of the story.

Mistakes are to be learned from and grown out of. They are opportunities for us to sheepishly, maybe, and humbly, definitively, turn back to God in search of the forgiveness or strength that will inevitably await us and help us to move on along a better path. One of the best lines in the New Testament dealing with failure comes in the story of the Prodigal Son, or the Forgiving Father as it is increasingly known. When the wayward son, who has really messed up, comes back to his father seeking forgiveness for his mistakes we read the following about the father's reaction to the son: 'He fell on his neck and kissed him.'

How wonderful to have a God who falls on our neck and kisses us when we mess up and ask for his forgiveness! And what better way to be his presence in the world than to do the same for others in our lives?

Meditation

Bring to mind the often unpleasant experience of failure, sit with it, try to find an image that captures it for you.

Admit your vulnerability in the face of this experience.

Acknowledge that you need God's help: make it real, not just asking a remote god but pleading with a living, breathing, concerned and compassionate God.

Make your own petition of what you need in your own words: 'God,' for example, 'I really screwed it up this time, I really can't cope and I desperately need some help.' Feel the weight of your need or desire in your words.

Picture Jesus on the Cross and try to connect emotionally with his awful pain and Passion, his whole project having failed, his friends having turned against him, having been betrayed by a friend, and abandoned by all but a few. He found a way though, abandoning himself to God (using the words of the Psalms: 'Into your hands O Lord'), by being faithful in prayer and believing against all odds that the power of God transformed this situation. All the violence, evil and hatred was transformed into forgiveness and compassion; death or disaster was not the end; in fact it was a new beginning.

Use your imagination to hand over your failure to Jesus to have it transformed; it takes complete trust and commitment.

Scripture

Luke 15:11–32 But while he was still far off, his father saw him and was filled with compassion; he ran and put his arms around him and kissed him.

Jeremiah 8:4 Thus says the Lord: When people fall, do they not get up again? If they go astray, do they not turn back?

Proverbs 3:5–6 Trust in the Lord with all your heart, and do not rely on your own insight. In all your ways acknowledge him, and he will make straight your paths.

Action

Write down your mistake on a piece of blank paper and fold it up. Light a small candle on the table in your sacred space. Place the folded sheet of paper in front of the candle as a way of bringing your mistake to God. Look at how the flame of the candle burns brightly and know that, even in your times of failure and mistakes, God's love burns for you even more intensely than the candle.

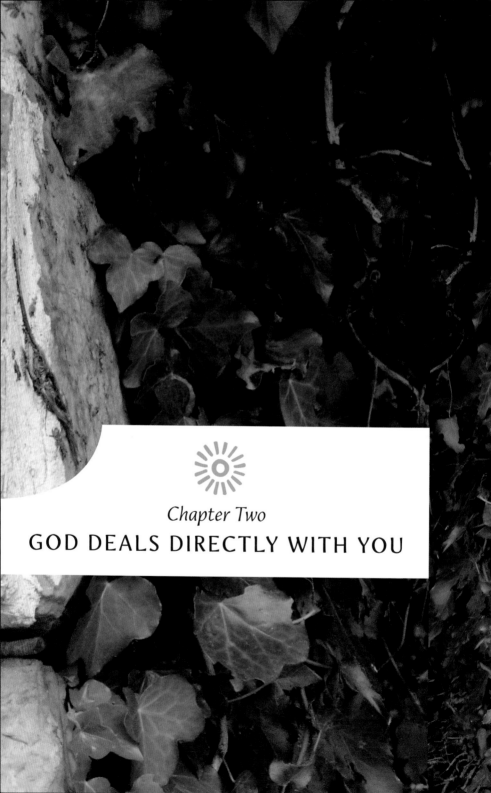

Chapter Two

GOD DEALS DIRECTLY WITH YOU

The Creator **deals directly** with the **creature,**
and the **creature deals directly** with the Creator.
Ignatius Loyola, *Spiritual Exercises #15*

CONVERSATION WITH GOD
Trust that God communicates directly with you

Me: Hello ... God?

God: Yes, my friend.

Me: God, I can't believe that you love me.

God: Really? Tell me about that, my friend.

Me: You can't. I've so many faults and failings. I'm broken in so many different ways.

God: My friend, what's going on?

Me: It's just, sometimes, God, I don't experience your love.

God: And do you think that because you don't experience it, it doesn't exist?

Me: Well, yeah. I don't feel it sometimes.

God: Tell me this, my friend, did you know that I created you, loved you into being, and do so every moment of the day?

Me: No. No, I didn't.

God: Tell me; what would it be like, my friend, if you were to live that inner beauty?

Me: Oh, I never thought of that. It would be life changing to realise that you were with me always. Just amazing.

God: So it is with my love for you, my friend. It changes you. It is total. It is awesome. It is awe-inspiring. It is life changing. It is already there. All you have to do is allow yourself to experience it.

Me: Well, how do I do that?

God: Be still and know that I am God. Be still and know that I am. Be still

and know. Be still. Be. Just take time each day simply to be who you are. But be who you are in the knowledge that I love you.

Me: *So are you saying that if I just spend a little bit of time every day acknowledging that you love me in silence and prayer that I'll experience your love?*

God: *Why don't you try? And why don't you look at the beautiful sunrise and sunset? And why don't you see the good people in your life? Why don't you see the good things that you have in your life? Why don't you see the forgiveness, the healing? All the signs of my love for you?*

Me: *God, I'll try.*

God: *You know, my friend, that would be a good start.*

Me: *A good start??*

God: *Yes, because once you experience my love, I need you to give it away to other people. But that's for another time.*

It's good to talk.

Praying in an Emergency

A friend struggling with mood swings hit some shocking lows in the past where he felt useless, despairing and unloved by all, including God. He talks about it now as a frightening experience, and about the hidden depths of the mind and extreme abandonment. He often thought about giving up on what he calls 'this hellish existence'. He often felt himself surrounded by darkness, threatened by despair and clinging on to faith by his fingernails. In these emergency situations he needed something to sustain him.

Trying to help him in these dark hours it was helpful to get him to focus on the positive, on his achievements and the people who love him; but this helped only a little.

The only thing that really worked was reminding him that Jesus was there for him, someone who knew similar pain, and that he himself didn't have to do anything to merit this love. Jesus who is pure love felt his pain, was with him in the darkness and wanted to bring comfort and relief. Most important for him to know was that he didn't have to do anything, didn't have to change or be different. It helped to alleviate the anxiety and tension he felt. It was an anchor in the storm.

Meditation

Breathe deeply and acknowledge that you need some help.

Picture Jesus looking at you – having an image of the 'shroud' or face of Jesus can be helpful here.

Try to see the love that he has for you personally, realise that he wants to help you, that he feels your pain.

Remember that he has been through the suffering on the Cross for you, he has only compassion for you.

He deeply desires to bring you some relief and some help – you can see it in his eyes.

Rest in his love, realise you are being held, that nothing can touch you here.

Speak to him about what is on your mind – tell him all your troubles, disappointments and suffering.

Listen to what he has to say to you, how he sees you, what hope he has for you and what he wants for you.

Resolve to put into practice any suggestions that come from the conversation.

Thank him for being there for you. Realise that you can pick up this conversation any time you need to.

Scripture

Isaiah 40:28–31 He gives power to the faint, and strengthens the powerless. Even youths will faint and be weary, and the young will fall exhausted; but those who wait for the Lord shall renew their strength, they shall mount up with wings like eagles, they shall run and not be weary, they shall walk and not faint.

Mark 14:32–42 And he said to them, 'I am deeply grieved, even to death; remain here, and keep awake.' And going a little farther, he threw himself on the ground and prayed, 'Abba, Father, for you all things are possible; remove this cup from me; yet, not what I want, but what you want.'

2 Corinthians 4:8–9 We are afflicted in every way, but not crushed; perplexed, but not driven to despair; persecuted, but not forsaken; struck down, but not destroyed.

Action

Call to mind your favourite image of Jesus. Breathe deeply to remind yourself you are not alone.

Take your time to look at the picture, notice the face of Jesus, his hair, his skin. Notice that his eyes are looking at you – Jesus is seeing you just as you are. He sees only the best in you and his look is one of great compassion and care. He wants you to know the great love that he has for you. Remind yourself that your pain or suffering is only temporary but his love is for ever. Stay with this exercise until you come to appreciate this love in your heart. Finish by giving thanks for what you have received, find the gratitude in your heart even if you don't always feel it. Place this picture in your sacred space; remember, you can come back to this at any time.

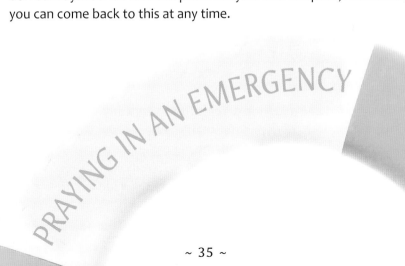

PRAYING IN AN EMERGENCY

Becoming Unstuck

One cold, bright spring morning a woman set about one of her core daily routines – hosing and clearing up her back garden. The sun was shining and the air was clear.

'This will be a cinch, working in these conditions,' she told herself.

She prepared the ground for hosing by shovelling and brushing and bleaching where necessary. Ten minutes in and she had a head of steam up – she was getting things done and it felt good. Next up was the hosing. Over she went to the outside water tap to which the hose was connected. She turned the tap on and ... nothing. She stood confused for a few seconds, looking from the tap to the nozzle of the hose, as if she could convince it into being by showing her confusion (and growing annoyance). She then shook the hose about a bit. Alas, that didn't work.

She went to walk away from the tap and as she did she stood on the hose. It made an unusual cracking sound. She stepped on another part of the hose and it made the same sound. In an instant she realised what the problem was – the hose was full of frozen water. The system was completely full and no more could be done.

'Well at least I know what the problem is,' she thought to herself. 'What can I do to fix it?'

What ensued was fifteen minutes of her walking on, twisting and shaking the hose about. She even poured hot water over it but she couldn't concentrate enough heat along the length of it to effect any change.

She stopped and admitted defeat. There was nothing she could do to make this hose work and get things done. As she stood there, a thought struck her. She remembered her earlier happiness at the fact that she would be working on a bright day. She looked up and saw the blue sky with a strong spring sun glowing in the middle of it, and the solution to her situation became clear.

Her job was to take a few minutes out and do nothing at all – even

though she felt a pressure to get things done. In ways she was like the hose; full to the brim with thoughts, plans, worries and the icy fear of getting nothing done.

All she had to do was let the sun do what it was doing all along – heating, easing and solving all the difficulties. She was just getting in the way and taking on too much responsibility. So she laid the hose down in and allowed the sun to do its gentle work. She had some breakfast and took some time to reflect on the wisdom she had encountered in this situation. In time, the hose thawed out and, well rested, she set about her work.

Meditation

Reread the story slowly and contemplate these four questions:

❈ Where in your life is it full to the point of being stuck?

❈ How could you take a step back from what you are doing and rest yourself?

❈ How might you acknowledge your reliance on others and on God in this situation?

❈ What might God be saying to you in this situation?

Matthew 11:28–30 'Come to me, all you that are weary and are carrying heavy burdens, and I will give you rest. Take my yoke upon you, and learn from me; for I am gentle and humble in heart, and you will find rest for your souls. For my yoke is easy, and my burden is light.'

Psalm 51:10 Create in me a clean heart, O God, and put a new and right spirit within me.

Matthew 6:13 And do not bring us to the time of trial, but rescue us from the evil one.

Action

Take an ice cube and place it in a glass. Hold the glass in your hands, cupping its edges. Watch as the ice cube begins to melt away in the glass. See how your sense of being stuck and tired can melt away in the heat of God's love for you.

Finding God in the Wilderness

The wilderness is a strong image. There are many different ways to imagine a wilderness. It could remind us, on the one hand, of walking in the countryside or in wide open spaces, with animals scurrying around about us in the sun or the rain. It could remind us of the silence of the many winding roads that don't seem to go any particular place, giving us time to think and pray. This is a positive experience of being in the wilderness. However, the wilderness can also be a place of desolation for us. It can be an internal landscape of worry, problems, sin and perceived distance from God. Being in the wilderness can be uncomfortable or worse.

Our job, it seems, is to bear with ourselves being in that wilderness. Wilderness times are inevitable parts of the story of life.

We see this in the Gospels when Jesus is driven into the wilderness. However, we are told that the wilderness was not the end of his journey. He emerged from that wilderness and came out the other side. Not only that, but he grew in the wilderness – he learned something about his life and his mission. We are told that he came out of the wilderness filled with the Spirit of God.

Emerging from the wilderness feels like a remote prospect when we are right in the middle of it. However, our emergence is as inevitable as the rising of the sun on a new day. We are invited to trust that God is with us in the wilderness and that we will emerge with deeper insights into ourselves, the world and our place in it. We need not worry or despair; it is God, after all, who ultimately straightens all paths out of the wilderness.

Meditation

Take a few deep, slow breaths and notice what happens to your body. As you breathe out, you will notice that your body falls slightly. You'll notice this in your chest or stomach. Then, when you breathe in deeply you will see your chest or stomach rise.

Call to mind times when we are more connected to the wilderness in the fall: sickness, loneliness, depression, addiction, relationship difficulties and more. Just as our bodies inevitably fall while we breathe out, they also inevitably rise again as we breathe in. Become conscious of these moments of rising on the in-breath, even in the midst of suffering. The rise moments are the times of mercy and compassion. They are the moments of genuine friendship and love and relief of suffering. They can also be the moments when others see us suffering with dignity. Ask yourself these questions:

- Where are my wilderness moments of experiencing the fall right now?
- What would I want to say to God about these moments?
- What would God say back to me?
- Where do I experience the sense of rising in my life right now?
- How can I be thankful and build on them?

Scripture

Mark 1:12–13 And the Spirit immediately drove him out into the wilderness. He was in the wilderness forty days, tempted by Satan; and he was with the wild beasts; and the angels waited on him.

Isaiah 43:19 I am about to do a new thing; now it springs forth, do you not perceive it? I will make a way in the wilderness and rivers in the desert.

Hosea 2:14 Therefore, I will now allure her, and bring her into the wilderness, and speak tenderly to her.

Action

Buy an old-fashioned egg timer. Watch how the sand moves from one part of the timer to the other as it is turned upside down. As it moves, become aware of the movement of God's Spirit within you and your own movement from the wilderness back into connectedness with yourself, with others and with God. You might like to place this egg timer in the sacred space in your home.

New Life (Dying and Rising)

Getting a new life seems so simple in the adverts: a new supplement, juicer or exercise machine promises a new body, energy and zest. If only it were so simple. The experience of many of us is that life is difficult and challenging and presents us with seemingly impossible situations of conflict, exclusion and hopelessness.

In fact, when we look back at those key moments of change, new life and genuine happiness in our lives, we notice that they were preceded by difficulty and burden to the point where we felt that we were dying, which is not a pleasant feeling. Things frequently have to get bad before we turn to God. There often has to be a death and dying (the Cross), before the new life of the resurrection is possible. Our lives often follow this cycle of dying and rising. Trying to control it is futile – we have to give ourselves to God in these moments.

Then we are thrown back on the only solid foundation we know – Jesus' experience on the Cross. It reminds us of the great love Jesus has for us in these tough situations, even if we don't feel it right now, and how we need to ask him to take our burdens and trust that he will transform them.

This is not an easy prayer but it reminds us of our desperate need of God, that we need to hand these situations over to God, and that it is only by the power of the resurrection that impossible situations get transformed. It is a lesson in humility, patience and pleading.

Meditation

Picture Jesus on the Cross and experience his great love for you personally. Give him your troubles and struggles, holding nothing back. Talk to him about your situation as one friend to another. Trust that God can work even in seemingly impossible situations.

Scripture

Luke 24:5 The women were terrified and bowed their faces to the ground, but the angels said to them, 'Why do you look for the living among the dead? He is not here, but has risen.'

John 7:38 And let the one who believes in me drink. As the scripture has said, 'Out of the believer's heart shall flow rivers of living water.'

Romans 6:4 Therefore we have been buried with him by baptism into death, so that, just as Christ was raised from the dead by the glory of the Father, so we too might walk in newness of life.

Action

Light a candle in a dark room. Watch the smoke and heat rising upwards. Realise that this is the reality of your relationship with God – new life comes through the fire and the flames. Give thanks for your life, even those tough moments where things have been difficult – this is where God works most powerfully.

Chapter Three

WHEN DARKNESS IS ALL AROUND

On each of my dyings shed your light and your love.
From the *Anima Christi*, Favourite prayer of Ignatius Loyola

CONVERSATION WITH GOD
Praying with difficult situations

Me: Hello … God?

God: Hello, my friend. It is so good to hear your voice. How are you?

Me: God, I'm having a bit of difficulty.

God: Tell me about it.

Me: Well, it's the whole praying thing …

God: Yes? How's that going?

Me: Well, that's the problem. It's not going at all.

God: In what way?

Me: I'm trying. I really am trying. But I just can't seem to get into it. I make all sorts of promises to make time to pray. But somehow I lose track of time or I get distracted. I feel awful.

God: It's ok to feel awful but, remember, I never seek that.

Me: Thank you. But I really do want to be able to pray. I even sit sometimes and begin to say my prayers. But it just feels stilted and then I give up.

God: Don't give up. I love a try-er, remember?

Me: So, you're really not angry?

God: No, my friend, I see that you are trying. And what are you doing right now?

Me: Right now? I'm sitting in my kitchen.

God: Yes. But what are you doing in your kitchen?

Me: I'm just sitting relaxing.

God: And??

Me: Talking to you.

God: There you go! Yes, you're talking to me. My friend, you're talking to me – talking to your God. My friend?

Me: Yes?

God: I hate to break it to you, but you're ... praying!

Me: I am? I am!

God: Yes, of course. Talking to me is a lovely and intimate way to pray. Don't get me wrong – I have given my people so many beautiful ways to pray. And the ways that you have been trying are beautiful as well. Keep trying. Prayer in any form can bring us closer together and that is my desire; for you to be united with me.

Me: And I want that too.

God: I know, my son. So many people do. So many want to be a good presence in my world. So many want to live well. So many want to help their fellow human beings, my friends. So many live to create a better world. And many of them do not even know or believe that I exist. And yet, their efforts, their very lives are prayers. And I hear them.

Me: So many ways to pray.

God: As many ways as there are people. That is my way.

Me: I will keep on trying. I will keep on talking to you. I will live my life so as to be a presence for good in your world. I will make this my prayer. Amen.

God: I hear your prayer. Amen.

It's good to talk.

Anxiety

Anxiety is difficult and painful. When it strikes it can be like the world becomes either very small to the point where it feels claustrophobic or so huge that it feels like we could lose ourselves completely. In many ways, suffering from anxiety is like having the very breath knocked out of us. Our bodies react in a similar way when we are anxious – our breathing becomes shallow and laboured; our bodies may become tense and ache all over; we may shake involuntarily. Our minds may become a hive of activity, and anxious minds play tricks on those of us who have them. Our minds tells us that all is lost, all is over and all is disaster. These are often just stories without basis in reality. But to those suffering from anxiety, they feel very real indeed.

Our spiritual and emotional life can also suffer when we are anxious. We can lose touch with ourselves and with our sense of a caring God.

How wonderful that we pray each time we gather as a community in the Mass that we would be free from distress – for distress, read anxiety. In fact, in the last translation of the Mass, the word anxiety was used rather than distress.

I think this is a reflection of the fact that anxiety is a common experience for all people. Ironically, though, when someone is in the grip of anxiety it can feel just the opposite – we feel like we are the only ones. We are not. We are not alone in our anxiety. As we see in the Mass, we can always rely on the peace, help and mercy of God to come to our aid in our distress and anxiety.

To counteract the breathlessness of anxiety, here are some ways to pray that can restore our breathing and our sense of calm in the reality of life and the real love that God has for us.

Meditation

Close your eyes and notice your breath. Don't try to change it at all; just notice it. If you notice it, you're alive! Just dwell on this for a while. Perhaps think to yourself, 'I am breathing. I am alive. I have life.'

Stay in this moment. If you find yourself wandering or judging yourself or others, just come back to your breath. Feel it go in and out of your body. Your body rises on the in-breath and falls on the out-breath. Feel the movement. And stay with your breath. As you do, become aware of your breaths becoming slightly longer and deeper. Do this for a full minute before reading on.

Take a few minutes now and notice the ebb and flow of your life.

Notice the easy times (here also read joyful times, playful times, peaceful times) and be truly thankful for them. Whatever your concept of God, I invite you, if you wish, to give some thanks to God for these times.

Now dedicate some space to the difficult times (here also read anxious times, sad times, disappointing times, shameful times and angry times). Notice them. Maybe you're in the middle of them right now. Maybe not. See them for what they are – yes, difficult, maybe even awful, but also temporary.

'All things pass.' Repeat this phrase as you breathe in and out for a minute or two.

Now, ask God to be with you in your anxious and difficult times. The guarantee is that God will be (and already is).

John 19:20–22 Jesus said to them again, 'Peace be with you. As the Father has sent me, so I send you.' When he had said this, he breathed on them and said to them, 'Receive the Holy Spirit.'

Psalm 94:19 When the cares of my heart are many, your consolations cheer my soul.

2 Thessalonians 3:16 Now may the Lord of peace himself give you peace at all times in all ways. The Lord be with all of you.

Action

Open the window or door of your home and allow the breeze (strong or light, it doesn't matter) to blow over you. As it does, call to mind the phrase from the Acts of the Apostles:

> Remember that Pentecost comes 'like a powerful wind from heaven, the noise of which filled the entire house'.

Experience the breeze from your window or door as the wind of the Holy Spirit blowing over you, bringing peace and freedom from anxiety.

Something on Suicide

The suicide of a loved one is devastating. All our support structures are kicked away and we can fall out of normal life and into a grim sort of survival. It is a grief journey like no other as it touches your deepest parts, especially your fears and crippling despairs. It demands everything from your personal resources of coping, emotional well-being and resilience. There is the initial shock of what has happened and the bizarre dream world that is the funeral, then there is the emptiness, the absence of the person and the pressing horror of the situation. Initially at least, shock is a helpful companion to isolate yourself from the pain.

There is often no chance to say goodbye, no closure, but rather the questions:

- ❄ Why did the person do it?
- ❄ Were we not enough?
- ❄ Why did we not see it coming?

We feel like screaming at God:

- ❄ How was this allowed to happen?
- ❄ If you are so powerful and the person was so good why did it end up bad?
- ❄ Where are they now and why can we not feel their presence?

These questions are all normal in the awful set of circumstances in which the bereaved find themselves.

As time goes by, the challenge for the suicide bereaved is to keep positive and hopeful even when things seem not to have moved on. It is like being reshaped in the depths of your humanity, painful but purifying, like gold that is tested in fire (1 P 1:7). It is common to experience some sort of faith crisis within yourself.

Eventually, slowly and over a long time, there will come a day when the pain will lessen. Others have survived and you will survive the storm of loss; calm will come eventually. But it is a hard road to

healing, a serious journey of survival in the face of hopelessness, despair and feelings of abandonment.

Jesus himself had the experience of feeling totally abandoned by God ('My God, My God, why have you forsaken me?' – Matthew 27:46) and feeling alone in the blackness of despair. Similarly, in our sharing in the Cross, God is with us in this darkest of hours, as the Father was with Christ in the garden, though hidden. In fact, Jesus accomplishes his most important mission, being faithful to love, feeling alone and deserted. Praying directly with your grief, even if you don't feel God's presence, helps to resolve it. It demands trust. It is crucial to believe that it is a God of compassion (meaning 'to suffer with us') who walks with you, especially through this darkest of nights.

Meditation

Take some time in a quiet and safe place where you know you can get the space to pray. Place yourself in the hands of God, humbly admitting that a solution is beyond yourself. Talk to Jesus directly about your struggle with darkness, despair and abandonment. Have your own conversation with God. Begin with, 'Father, into your hands I commend my spirit' (Lk 23:46).

Let your conversation flow. As you speak to God, the important thing to remember is that Christ loves you exactly as you are, even if you feel like a mess. The saying 'Pray as you are and not as how you want to be' is helpful, just give it all to God.

Allow yourself to experience guilt, hopelessness and despair; just acknowledging them is enough. If you are angry with God, let God have it – God can handle it. God is with us in everything, even if we don't feel close to him. See God looking at you with great compassion.

Meditate like this for a maximum of twenty minutes before going on with your day. A little time spent in meditation each day can be helpful if done gently and without pressure.

Scripture

Isaiah 53:3–5 But he was wounded for our transgressions, crushed for our iniquities; upon him was the punishment that made us whole, and by his bruises we are healed.

Psalm 22:1 My God, my God, why have you forsaken me?

John 12:27 'Now my soul is troubled. And what should I say –"Father, save me from this hour?" No, it is for this reason that I have come to this hour.'

Action

Select a symbol of the person you have lost, something that evokes them strongly, such as a piece of clothing, a photo, a personal item. Make a simple pilgrimage to a place you associate with that person. Carry your symbol with you on this pilgrimage. Walk to a special place, climb a mountain, swim a certain number of lengths in a pool, cycle a route that is special for you. Prepare a ritual action that has meaning for you, such as holding a photo of the person, writing a grief 'journal', remembering some special times with your beloved, or prayerfully honouring their passing by composing a prayer in your own words. You may have to repeat this process a number of times, adjusting certain elements as you go. Notice where you might be getting stuck and pray for help with that part.

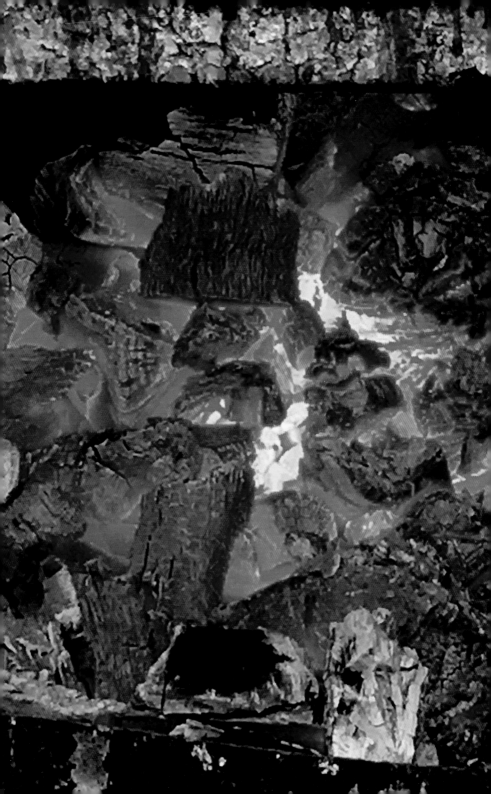

Anger

Anger is a gift from God. This can sound surprising, shocking even, as so many people struggle with anger and frustration, often feeling they live under a heavy cloud of resentment. We need only look at Jesus clearing the Temple (Jn 2:13–22) to realise how he uses anger effectively and appropriately to correct a wrong (trading and selling) that had crept into this sacred place.

Anger is a volatile and fiery emotion; it can flare quickly, easily dominate our thinking and take over our minds and actions to the point where it comes out as harsh, ugly and damaging. The problem is that incorrectly used it is hijacked by our emotions, not used for God's plan.

If the purpose of anger is to right a wrong, then we have to be careful to use it appropriately and to direct it at the problem. Many people end up carrying enormous amounts of unexpressed anger because of real or perceived hurts, or end up letting fly at anyone or anything that gets in the way (I see red and let go so all around me feel the anger).

Praying with anger is enormously difficult because of the amount of emotion involved.

Meditation

Find a quiet place where you can be alone and undisturbed, and try to calm your breathing. One of the first steps is to talk openly and honestly to God about what you feel. Let God have it and hold nothing back. God can handle this. This helps take some of the sting out of the emotion.

Explore the source of your anger. Ask yourself:

✳ What am I reacting against?

✳ How might I be fooled by the emotion and could I be misled into doing something rash?

✳ What options are available to me for how I could express the anger in a healthy way?

✳ What would be the most effective way of doing this?

Asking 'How would God want me to express this?' can help turn down the emotional heat so that another person can hear the words and choose how to act. It is the difference between aggression and assertion; Jesus knew how to combine love and criticism in a powerful way. Sometimes we come to a point where we don't need to express our anger; we can move beyond it. So we can ask ourselves, am I able to let it go and let God?

Scripture

John 2:13–22 Making a whip of cords, he drove all of them out of the Temple, both the sheep and the cattle. He also poured out the coins of the money changers and overturned their tables. He told those who were selling the doves, 'Take these things out of here! Stop making my Father's house a marketplace!'

Ephesians 4:26–28 In your anger do not sin: Do not let the sun go down while you are still angry, and do not give the devil a foothold. Anyone who has been stealing must steal no longer, but must work, doing something useful with their own hands, that they may have something to share with those in need.

Proverbs 14:29 Whoever is slow to anger has great understanding, but one who has a hasty temper exalts folly.

Action

Go to a lonely or remote place, even use a car or empty room, to shout and scream to God. Use your whole body to express how you are feeling and pray to God about the anger you are feeling; use your hands, fists and your whole body to express the emotion – give it all to God, holding nothing back, knowing that this is a safe and good place for you to be angry. Understand that sometimes you can be angry with God also and that you need to have it out between you to clear the air.

Self-criticism

There was once a young girl who loved to draw. She loved the feeling of the pens and pencils in her hands. She loved the feeling of making marks on the page. When she walked around the town where she lived, she saw pictures everywhere. She drew animals; she drew people; she drew houses; she drew cars; she drew trees. And she drew very well.

But a strange thing happened every time she finished a picture. Almost as soon as she looked at the beautiful bright colours she had drawn, they began to change into greys and blacks and the picture looked like a jumbled mess. At that point, she got very sad and very down on herself.

'I am a terrible drawer. And this drawing is ugly,' she would say, as she stuffed the ugly drawing into her bottom drawer along with all the other ugly drawings she had done. After a while, she got so sad about the ugly drawings that she stopped seeing her town as being full of scenes just waiting to be drawn and she drew less and less.

Many years went by and the young girl grew up to be a woman. Every now and then, she would try to draw something, but the same thing would happen. She would draw something beautiful, but it would change into an ugly drawing. This happened so many times that she eventually gave up.

And so the woman grew old and sad and, eventually, she died.

Her house was sold to a young couple who had a daughter. When they moved into the house, the old woman's furniture was still inside. The daughter explored her new house and found the room where the old woman had put the chest of drawers with the drawings inside. She opened one drawer at a time until she came to the bottom drawer. When she saw the drawings, she called out to her parents, 'Mummy, daddy, come here. I have found such beautiful drawings. They have grand colours and wonderful straight lines and curves and they are magnificent. This must have been the house of a great artist!'

Remember you too have a great talent – a light to shine forth just like the woman in the story. Perhaps it is singing, or writing, or being a great listener, or sewing, or being a friend, or being a parent or grandparent, or being an uncle or aunt, or cooking delicious food. Don't hide your talent away. Share it with the world. Don't be hard on yourself – we are often the worst judges of our own abilities.

Meditation

Read the story slowly again. Focus on the characters. With which of the characters in the story do you associate most?

※ Is it the self-critical artist?

※ Is it the little girl who was able to see the giftedness that the artist could not?

※ Is it the parents who were there in the background supporting the little girl to be curious and to find the giftedness in their house (in the world)?

※ Is it a combination of these?

Spend some time in silence and contemplate what it is about those characters that you identify with. When an insight arises, speak to God about it. Wonder what God's invitation to you might be.

Matthew 5:16 In the same way, let your light shine before others, so that they may see your good works and give glory to your Father in heaven.

Proverbs 19:8 To get wisdom is to love oneself; to keep understanding is to prosper.

John 15:9 As the Father has loved me, so I have loved you; abide in my love.

Action

Take a blank sheet of paper. Marvel at its newness and the possibility it holds as it waits for the mark of a pen or pencil. Write on that sheet of paper at least one gift you have (write as many as you want). Don't let yourself off the hook; we all have a gift or two, even if we've hidden them or not noticed them for a while. Here's a list to help you get started: Singing, writing, praying, listening to others, being generous with time or money, drawing, making good decisions, encouraging others, putting others first, suffering with humility, biting your lip.

Once you have written on your piece of paper, put it in a sacred space in your home. Return to this list on days when you feel self-critical.

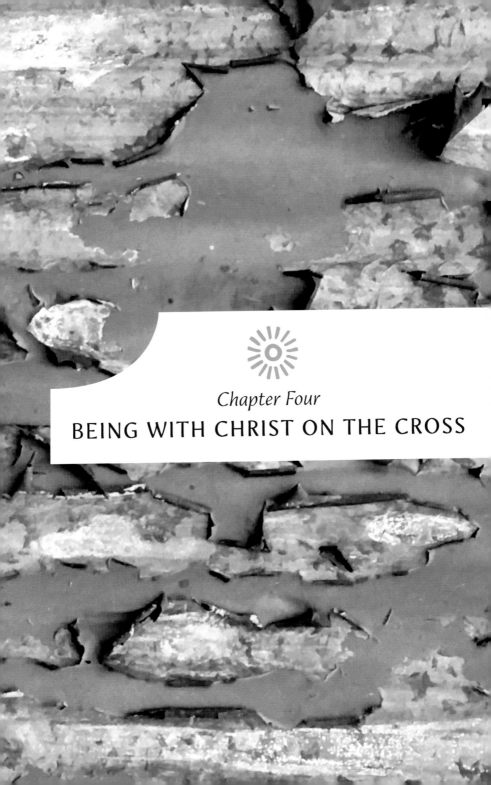

Chapter Four

BEING WITH CHRIST ON THE CROSS

Imagine Christ our Lord present
before you upon the cross,
and begin to speak with him.
Ignatius Loyola, *Spiritual Exercise* no 53

CONVERSATION WITH GOD
Fear

Me: *Hello ... God?*

God: *Hello, my friend. What's going on?*

Me: *I find myself worrying a lot about the future. Like, what's going to happen in the future?*

God: *Maybe that's why you haven't talked to me in a while?*

Me: *Probably. Sorry.*

God: *I forgive you. Tell me more.*

Me: *Sometimes I wonder where I am going and where my life is leading. I start to make really elaborate plans for the future, usually based on avoiding something going wrong.*

God: *And how is that working out for you?*

Me: *Not so well. I get mentally tongue tied in all these plans. And mostly, they don't work out like I planned anyhow.*

God: *I know the hope I have for you. This is me speaking to you now. I know you better than you know yourself. And let that be enough for you. If I'm watching out for you, you don't have to worry.*

Me: *That's a relief in a way. But in another, it's a worry. Making plans makes me feel in control.*

God: *And are you?*

Me: *In control? Well ... no.*

God: I am. Let that be a comfort to you.

Me: I will.

God: What will you do with all that time you'll have, now you're not planning too much?

Me: I'll live for today, every day. And I'll talk to you more.

God: Good! I look forward to that.

It's good to talk.

Fear

A friend of mine is a professional in the computer industry but suffers a lot with fear whenever he has to give a presentation, which often happens. Before the presentation he is plagued by doubts and fears about what might go wrong: what if he is not good enough, or feels out of his depth professionally or if something goes wrong? He is tempted to pull out of the presentation, making an excuse to avoid the situation to reduce the fear.

But somehow, he knows that it would be good for him to do it, that he is able to do it and that he will feel better afterwards. He always has a great feeling of peace and achievement when he faces his fears. He has learned to pray with his fears and that helps to get him through. He is a successful person despite the fears that are present every time he plans a presentation.

Fear has a very powerful negative effect on us, although it is sometimes useful in protecting us from situations of danger. However, it is mostly something that cripples and paralyses, leaving us unable to act or move forward. It imprisons us. Even though it is safe, it is airless and isolating. We are isolated because of fear. The tragedy is that we don't get to use our God-given talents and the world is poorer for that.

Meditation

Fear, while having a positive role in warning us of danger, is not a good counsellor. It promises safety and security by not taking any risks, but it leads only to a sterile isolation.

Take some time to pray with the problem, acknowledging that excessive fear is not what God wants and asking for help to overcome it. Pray for a specific grace or gift from God, the ability to overcome fear in order that we can carry out God's will and use our gifts in the service of others.

Ask for the spirit of courage and bravery to fill your heart with love and help drive out fear. Realise that you are more than your feelings, and that your spirit of courage within you will win out. Ask yourself these questions:

✳ What are your gifts and talents?

✳ What is the fear or block that cripples you?

✳ How can you pray with this – what is the specific grace you need?

Scripture

John 14:27 Peace I leave with you; my peace I give to you. I do not give to you as the world gives. Do not let your hearts be troubled, and do not let them be afraid.

Isaiah 43:1 Do not fear, for I have redeemed you; I have called you by name, you are mine.

Psalm 23:4 Even though I walk through the darkest valley, I fear no evil; for you are with me; your rod and your staff, they comfort me.

Action

Find a quiet place inside or outside your house. Take a deep breath and hold it for a few seconds. Feel your chest fill up with air. Feel the tightness in your muscles. Experience this as the fullness of God's love for you. Breathe out and say confidently, 'I will not fear. God is with me.'

Repeat this as many times as you wish.

Addiction

An addict is often someone who is searching for God, in the wrong places, maybe, but with a powerful need for the transcendent, beauty and a deeper meaning to help them recover. The fixation on drink, drugs, gambling or an escape is often a good desire gone bad, one that has focused on a lesser thing and missed the Creator of all things. Complex psychological and physical factors can contribute to addiction, and the journey back to some sort of functioning is very difficult and fraught. Many addicts find solace and comfort in the mercy and acceptance of Christ's loving gaze, and can find great strength and fortitude in prayer.

Most of us are mercifully free of being overly attached to any thing or individual, to be able to use (or not) the good things of the world. Unfortunately, that is not a reality for those who suffer from addictions of one type or other, whether to alcohol, gambling, drugs or sex. The list is almost endless as the target for our desires can literally be anything in the world. St Augustine has a great line:

> You were within me, but I was outside, and it was there that I searched for you. In my unloveliness I plunged into the lovely things which you created. You were with me, but I was not with you. Created things kept me from you; yet if they had not been in you they would have not been at all.

It is often a search for God that is frustrated and diverted into lesser things, that although created by God, mistakenly become the centre of one's world. Apparently addicts struggle with the delusion that these 'God-created' things will bring us to God, and fall on them to solve their inner desires and cravings. Many addicts say they found God precisely in their struggle, learning about their own weakness and vulnerability and utter dependence on God. Unfortunately, the consequence of their lesser choices is great suffering, lives spent in pursuit of these false gods, health destroyed, families split apart,

reputations in tatters. Sometimes it is only in God that this devastation can be redeemed or at least offer hope of a better life.

St Ignatius says that God is in our deepest desires for love, belonging and acting with love, not in the superficial ones of likes or wants. Nowhere is this more true than in the area of addiction, where a good desire is twisted and thwarted into something ugly and bitter. However, it is still a desire for God. The person, the addict, is still a beloved of God. Regardless of what they have done, there is a path back to life and love. Often the sense of guilt and shame sits very heavy on them and they often feel that God has abandoned them or sits in judgement on them.

Just as in AA, the fundamental starting point is that they are not in control of their lives and that there is a 'higher power'. This is not an impersonal judge however, but a compassionate parent who longs for the return of their child. They need to admit their absolute unworthiness and dependency on God to be able to move forward. This is a lot more difficult that it sounds. Addicts know the chaos they have wreaked on themselves and others and so easily fall into bitterness, hurt and guilt ... but these emotions, though understandable, are not from God. There is a fundamental blessedness or goodness in all human beings that the world cannot touch. It lies deep within us, unnoticed and unexplored.

Meditation

This is the hardest prayer of all, to believe against all the evidence that I am a friend of God, that despite all the mistakes I have made, the Father welcomes me home. It is the ultimate Prodigal Son or Daughter story, taking up one's face from the pigs' trough and remembered that there is a place where I am loved and that I can call home. Then I have to make the journey back there, knowing that I have squandered away the riches I have been given and that I am no longer worthy to be called a son or daughter. Yet, miraculously, I am received with open arms – the Father almost crushes me in an embrace and showers me with kisses. It's all too much. However, it is a journey that I have to make many times, it is a prodigal that slips and falls continually, and have to believe that there is still a way back. The key is the remembering of who I am, my prior dignity and worth in God's eyes.

Scripture

Luke 15:11–32 But when he came to himself he said, 'How many of my father's hired hands have bread enough and to spare, but here I am dying of hunger!

2 Corinthians 5:17 Therefore, if anyone is in Christ, the new creation has come: The old has gone, the new is here!

Luke 6:37 'Do not judge, and you will not be judged; do not condemn, and you will not be condemned. Forgive, and you will be forgiven.'.

Action

* Find a quiet space where you can be alone and not be disturbed.
* Pray for the grace that you need to acknowledge the harm you have done to yourself and others, ask for God's healing and forgiveness and find a path of healing.
* Begin by acknowledging your feelings, whatever they are. Write them out on a page or speak them to God, be real.
* Use your body to express how you feel about your life: prostration or lying on the floor can help to express what is in you. Express your helplessness before God.
* Express your sorrow or regret, acknowledge that you have done wrong.
* Beg for the gift of healing; imagine God welcoming you home and embracing you, what would it feel like to be forgiven?
* Go for a long walk, praying for the grace of forgiveness and healing.
* Commit yourself to concrete actions to reform your life; ask for the help you need.

Lost

He had done it again! He and his wife had taken their young family to the country where, after having been out for a forest walk, he took a wrong turn when driving back to the holiday house they were staying in. That one wrong turn took him and his family on a journey of about sixty extra miles and changed their plans for the afternoon.

They were all cold and wet from their forest walk and wanted to get back to the house to heat up, change clothes and have a bite to eat. As they went down the wrong road and he realised that they weren't going home, he started to get frustrated. He could see no good in this journey they were taking. It only took them away from where they wanted to go – where HE wanted to go. And it was uncomfortable because he no longer felt in control. As the road went on out into the deepest wilderness, he got down on himself. 'I'm spoiling the kids' afternoon', he told himself. He silently fumed for a few more miles. Then he began to look around a bit as he drove along. They were indeed lost, and in the middle of absolutely nowhere. But … it was gorgeous!

The hills and mountains stretched as far as the eye could see on one side of the car. On the other side the fields stretched down to a massive lake. He realised they were in the middle of 'God's country'. He breathed deeply, gave himself a mental hug, told God that he gave up control and just drove on. Suddenly being lost was actually fun. They came across more and more beautiful sights. What had been a bit of a disaster now became an adventure. He let go of the need to control his destination and just … journeyed. After a while he saw a sign for a town he recognised and got back on track. The afternoon ended with a walk on a beach and chips for dinner for the kids.

This story is the stuff of life itself. Life can occur to us as an uncomfortable journey. We can even feel lost at times. In these times it isn't so much about what we do to regain our direction that counts, but what we are willing to let God do. We can get so caught up that

we miss the little moments of beauty and relief that we are given along the way. Life can seem all wilderness. But that is never the whole story. Bad times end. This is not to patronise you or minimise the difficulties you face. It is simply a statement of reality and of hope. The bad times end.

Meditation

What journey in your life are you on right now? Name it. Where do you experience feeling lost? Name it. Breathe in and say, 'Lord, I feel lost'. Breathe out and say, 'Lord, I let you find me'. *Repeat for a few minutes.*

Scripture

Jeremiah 29:11 For surely I know the plans I have for you, says the Lord, plans for your welfare and not for harm, to give you a future with hope.

Romans 8:38 For I am convinced that neither death, nor life, nor angels, nor rulers, nor things present, nor things to come, nor powers,

Luke 15:4 'Which one of you, having a hundred sheep and losing one of them, does not leave the ninety-nine in the wilderness and go after the one that is lost until he finds it?'

Action

Buy or find a small toy car. Place it in your sacred space to remind you that it is God, and not you, who is in the driving seat. God will always find the best way forward for you if you can let go of control.

Outsiders

People from foreign parts, or outsiders, are often seen as problems these days. We get a false sense from the news about Europe being flooded with immigrants and countries being unable to cope with the influx. The response has often been to build walls and barriers to keep them out, just like the walls and barriers we build in our hearts. We can harden our hearts against others, not really seeing them as human or even remotely like ourselves, rather justifying harsh treatment and hostility. Also, we can justify ourselves as being good people, Christians even, without having to deal with others or those that are different. After all, we tell ourselves, 'God created this land for us, for our people and race, and we are the favoured people, to the exclusion of others … '.

Except this is all wrong. In fact, it's the opposite of what Christianity is about in terms of welcoming the stranger, helping those in difficulty and having basic human compassion. At the heart of it is the idea that we are created by God, that is all of us are created by God, and everyone has the right to dignity and life. There is a famous song by REM called 'Everybody Hurts', which points to a fundamental solidarity, that all of us feel emotions and can be hurt, regardless.

Looking at Jesus in the Gospels we see someone who goes out of his way to include outsiders: greeting the tax collector, prostitute, sinner, outsider, leper, non-Jew. It really is striking that Jesus condemns all those who are closed and narrow in relation to others, especially the religious authorities of the day, and shows the essence of Christianity to be welcoming, inclusive, reaching out to all. The parable of the Good Samaritan was shocking for Jews because it was so unthinkable in Palestine to help non-Jews. Jesus keeps on rocking the boat in a continual series of seeing good in outsiders and welcoming them, against all perceived wisdom.

Meditation

❈ Breathe deeply and pray for openness to others who are different.

❈ Picture Jesus looking at you; try to see the love that he has for you personally, realise that he wants you to be open to others, to bring his love to outsiders.

❈ Remember how Jesus was always there for people who were different or outcast, how do you think he was able to do that? Imagine yourself so totally given over to God's love that kindness and compassion ooze out of you.

❈ What would your life be like if you were to live like that? Who are the outsiders that you come across?

❈ Talk to Jesus about how he wants you to live, what he wants for you, and tell him about any resistances or blocks you find in yourself.

❈ Resolve to put into practice any suggestions that come from the conversation. Thank him for being there for you.

Scripture

Luke 10:25–37 'Which of these three, do you think, was a neighbour to the man who fell into the hands of the robbers?' He said, 'The one who showed him mercy.' Jesus said to him, 'Go and do likewise.'

Exodus 23:9 You shall not oppress a stranger, since you yourselves know the feelings of a stranger, for you also were strangers in the land of Egypt.

Colossians 4:5 Conduct yourselves wisely toward outsiders, making the most of the time.

Action

Pick someone you meet on the street, see on TV or especially someone that you have an aversion to. Try to imagine what it would like to meet them; try to see beyond the exterior skin colour, clothes, appearance or accent. Imagine you could see right through to their heart, what might they be feeling? What kind of emotions might be to the fore? Anger, fear, happiness, unease, concern or grief are just some of the endless possibilities.

Imagine how God would see them: picture God's unique care for them, God's dream for them and their life. What aspect of God's creation can you see in them: humour, confidence, difference, pride, adaptability, love of family etc.?

What could you do to connect with them? Sometimes a smile or nod is enough to acknowledge people and says, 'I see you, I'm glad you're here, keep on going'. Sometimes a hug is all that is needed.

Recovery from a Breakdown

There is little that is more frightening than a breakdown, a meltdown in human functioning, hitting a wall at speed, being reduced to a nervous wreck and sometimes needing psychiatric help. It is the ultimate humbling of a person, to have to admit that you can't cope, that you need help and that you have to step back from the normal commitments of life, family, relationships and job.

Truth be told, initially there can be a huge sense of relief when you get some rest, feel protected and get the problem out in the open. Then follows the creeping acceptance, possibly embarrassment and then the sense of failure or disaster – a life ruined?

Rebuilding is hard work – the therapy, facing unpleasant aspects of yourself, taking responsibility for what led to the crisis (perhaps overwork, rigidity of mind or body, depression or anxiety?). As well as the recovery, there is extra energy needed for facing oneself squarely and honestly and working out what has to change to live life better. Medication and meditation are uncomfortable companions but one needs the other.

It's hard to keep believing in a good God and that you are worth something after such a 'fall'. The embarrassment, shame and pain of it all can be a real barrier to healing. Taken positively, however, it can be the impulse to rebuild myself, fix faults and imagine a new life. Your spiritual life is central, as well as all the therapy and medicine. You may need to overhaul faulty ideas about God as harsh and demanding, or yourself as too work focused, living the damaging delusion of being a 'superhero' or simply neglectful of the basic human necessities of rest, companionship and laughter.

The good news is that recovery is possible and a new life in Christ is promised for those who are true to the process of rebuilding the body, mind and spirit. Halfway solutions won't do though – I have to let the light into all those dark areas that have had such power over me and give myself totally over to God in a new way. It is the total

abandonment modelled by Jesus on the Cross – acceptance that my life is a failure and my only hope is in God as I trust myself completely to the resurrection of hope within me.

With today's modern medicine, psychology and therapy, a full recovery is possible, but what's sometimes missed is that it's the Spirit that ties all these strands together and makes for a new heart. It's not just an optional extra or therapeutic add-on, but it is the crucial glue that binds and holds everything in place.

Imagine how differently you will live after this experience, how you will put this hard-earned wisdom into being a better person, being more compassionate and kind and recognising pain and suffering in others.

Your new prayer has to be focused on recovery – praying the Psalms for help in distress, the healing stories of Jesus for therapy and the ongoing 'conversation with God' as a guide for decisions.

Meditation

✳ Use a psalm, e.g. Psalm 139, to place yourself before God exactly as you are – make it real. Use a healing story from the Gospels to bring Jesus' healing to bear on that part of your life that is broken; ask directly for what you want, be bold. Use the story about the woman with haemorrhages (Luke 8:43–48) who was desperate to touch Jesus. Imagine yourself having that level of desperation. See yourself trying to get close to Jesus, maybe just to touch the edge of his cloak. Maybe there is much shame and embarrassment and you don't want to be seen. But then Jesus notices, and turns around to ask who touched him – he looks right into your eyes – what do you feel? How does he look at you, what does he want for you and what do you have to do to make yourself known or ask for help. Practise saying the words of a prayer for healing like these: 'It was me Jesus, I touched your cloak out of desperation but now I am afraid; I really want to be healed but I find myself unable to do it alone, I really need your help.' Continue the conversation; talk to Jesus as one friend to another about your life, challenges and what you really need, ask for what you want and be open to hear what you need. Take as long as you need.

☀ Close with a prayer of thanks; work out what practical steps you need for your further healing.

Scripture

Psalm 139:7–12 Where can I go from your spirit? Or where can I flee from your presence? If I ascend to heaven, you are there; if I make my bed in Sheol, you are there.

Jeremiah 29:11 'For surely I know the plans I have for you,' says the Lord, 'plans for your welfare and not for harm, to give you a future with hope.'

Matthew 9:20–22 A woman who had been bleeding for twelve years came up behind Jesus and sought to touch him.

Action

Take an old piece of your clothing that is torn or damaged. Take the time to darn it yourself, using a needle and thread to stitch together the jagged edges. Notice how you feel as you do this. What emotions come up within you? When you have finished (it doesn't have to be pretty or neat), see how strong the garment has become. Realise that even if it has a mended tear, it is strong and usable; it can be useful and whole again. It is a special scar or wound that you wear.

Chapter Five

GOD TURNS EVERYTHING TO THE GOOD

'The grace to be glad and to rejoice intensely.'
Ignatius Loyola, *Spiritual Exercises* #221

CONVERSATION WITH GOD
Do you love messy me?

Me: Hello, God?

God: Hello, my friend. What's up?

Me: Do you love me?

God: I do.

Me: Thank you. See you later.

God: Not so quick. You haven't spent time with me for a while, so don't rush away.

Me: Yes, of course. Sorry.

God: No need for an apology. It's great to spend time with you. I wonder why you asked me that question though; why you asked if I love you?

Me: Oh, just wondering, that's all …

God: Ok. I've a question for you.

Me: Do you not know everything?

God: Yes, I know everything. But I'm not asking you a question for me to find out the answer. I'm asking so you will find it.

Me: Oh, right. What's the question?

God: Do you love you?

Me: Oh. Umm … Yeah?

God: You don't sound convinced, my friend.

Me: I haven't thought about that for a while. I do love bits of me.

God: Which bits are those?

Me: The good bits.

God: And which bits are those?

Me: The bits that do well and make good decisions and get it right.

God: The bits you show mostly to the world?

Me: Yes. I suppose. Yes, you're right.

God: But what about those other bits, my friend? The bits underneath what the world sees.

Me: I don't always love them.

God: How do those bits feel?

Me: Messy.

God: Yes, they are. But you know what?

Me: Yes, God?

God: I love the messiness as well.

Me: You do?

God: Yes, and I want you to see it and love it too. Bring your messiness to me. Let's talk about it. Let's look at it. Let's love it together. And in loving it, you will be transformed.

Me: That's a tough one. But I will try.

God: And I will be with you. Go in peace.

It's good to talk.

Messy Family Life

A friend was thinking about family a while ago as he carved a spoon out of a mahogany block in his workshop out in the garage. In the midst of cutting and gouging and filing, the thought struck him that families are really important. He tells us it was because, as he stood in his garage working, he could see in through the kitchen window as his wife read a book and his daughter did her homework and his sons were eating – again! That's family on a Saturday afternoon!

Families provide us with a lot of comfort and security. But it could be easy to get caught up in wanting our family to be like that all the time or to be somehow 'perfect'. If we think that families are places where everything goes right all the time and nothing goes wrong, or where people always get things right, then we're setting ourselves up for a fall. And we're missing the point.

Family life is messy because people are messy. Life is messy. It doesn't always go right. However, in families, the mistake can be forgiven and the people loved despite, or even because of, their mistakes. The genius of family does not lie in never messing up or in getting it right all the time, but in its being a place where the possibility of true love and commitment to each other is always alive. This is what makes it sacred space.

Back in the garage our friend was almost finished making the spoon, but he messed up and broke it! It was absolutely lovely up to that point – perfect even. But one glance too many with the file and the spoon was broken. Now, our friend says that he could have become very angry or very down on himself or even on the wood for not being strong enough; for not being perfect.

But then he remembered that he was carving this spoon whilst reflecting on the imperfect and messy nature of families. It caused him to wonder,

'What do we do when we encounter brokenness in our families? What would God have us do?'

God would have us love the brokenness and broken person and in that love to transform that which was broken into something beautiful.

So he set about transforming the broken. He looked at the bowl of the spoon and turned it upside down. He fashioned the handle into four legs and a wee head. And it became ... a tortoise! Yes, he carved the broken pieces into a little tortoise. While it is shaped differently from what it had originally been, it is, nevertheless a lovely thing that sits on the sacred space in his living room and brings a smile to those who see it.

Families are our backbone. They give us a sense of where we came from and where we are going. Families create homes. And homes can be places of love, nurturing and welcome. They are places where we can tolerate mess and celebrate our difference, and where we gather round one truth – we are all created by a loving God whose love for us knows no limits and who wants our families to be an expression of Church, of the Gospels and of the Joy of Love itself.

Meditation

Families come in all shapes and sizes. Name some of the members of your immediate and extended family. Name them one by one and, as you do, take a moment to pray for that family member – especially the members who are a bit messy or who cause you to feel a bit messy. Breathe deeply as you do this. Ask God to be with you in the messiness of everyday family life and in any particularly distressing family situation you or a loved one are facing.

Ephesians 2:19–22 You are no longer strangers and aliens, but you are citizens with the saints and also members of the household of God, built upon the foundation of the apostles and prophets, with Christ Jesus himself as the cornerstone.

Colossians 3:13 Bear with one another and, if anyone has a complaint against another, forgive each other; just as the Lord has forgiven you, so you also must forgive.

1 Corinthians 13:4–7 Love is patient; love is kind; love is not envious or boastful or arrogant or rude. It does not insist on its own way; it is not irritable or resentful; it does not rejoice in wrongdoing, but rejoices in the truth. It bears all things, believes all things, hopes all things, endures all things.

Action

Find an object that speaks to you of the goodness of your family life. For our friend in this story, it was the little tortoise. It can be whatever you want. Find the object and put it in your sacred space in your home. Go to it when family life is messy and allow it to remind you of God's love for you and your family.

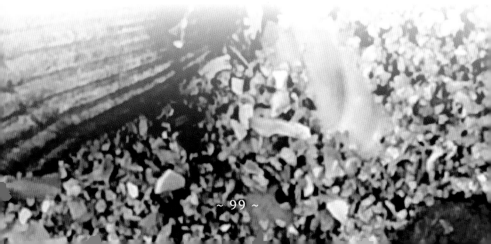

Finding Hope

To feel hopeless is to feel like a boat tossed about on a violent sea in the dead of night. We feel that we have lost control of any positive direction our life could take. Any moments of calm are often accompanied by feelings of emptiness or dread. In the midst of hopelessness it becomes difficult to make good choices or even to make any choices at all. We feel like that boat being thrown this way and that, with no sense of our own ability to set a good course.

Most people experience moments of hopelessness along life's journey. There are of course those who experience it more than most. What are we to do if we are caught in the swirling sea of hopelessness?

Here's an interesting quote from St Augustine: 'The Lord has shed his blood, redeemed us, changed our hope … on the sea we are tossed by the waves, but we have the anchor of hope already fixed upon the land.'

It seems that Augustine knew what it meant to be all at sea. It is also clear that he knew that there was another way to see life, to see hope. He spoke of a changed hope; a hope he recognised in God's great love for us all. He describes that hope as being and anchor fixed to the land – the promised land perhaps!

Meditation

Hopelessness disconnects us from the reality of who we are and the reality of God's great love for us. Let's spend a few minutes reconnecting to all of this.

❀ Sit or lie in a comfortable position. Become aware of your body. Trace an imaginative line right up from your toes to the top of your head, stopping off at all your major muscles along the way. Feel them relax and feel your body become heavier. With this sensation become aware of being alive in the present moment.

❀ Now breathe deeply. On your out-breath say aloud, 'Everything will be ok.' Repeat as often as it takes for this sentence to take root.

Scripture

Mark 4:35–41 He woke up and rebuked the wind, and said to the sea, 'Peace! Be still!' Then the wind ceased, and there was a dead calm. He said to them, 'Why are you afraid? Have you still no faith?'

Genesis 8:1 But God remembered Noah and all the wild animals and all the domestic animals that were with him in the ark. And God made a wind blow over the earth, and the waters subsided;

1 Peter 1:3 Blessed be the God and Father of our Lord Jesus Christ! By his great mercy he has given us a new birth into a living hope through the resurrection of Jesus Christ from the dead.

Action

Choose an object you associate with good times, love and hope. For some this might be a flower or a picture of a rainbow. It can be whatever you choose. Place this in a sacred place in your home. Visit it often and allow it to remind you of the hope that God's love brings for all of us. Remember, everything will be all right in the end. If it's not all right, it's not the end.

Facing Death

The last words of St Ignatius Loyola are said to have been, 'Oh, my God!' (cf. *The First Jesuit*). He uttered them at the start of the final journey he was about to undertake – a journey out of the mess of this world and into the perfection of eternal rest in the arms of a loving God.

Facing our own death we ask a number of questions. One common question is, 'What will happen to me?'

As St Ignatius faced his death, might he have said the words, 'Oh, my God!' in joyful surprise at just how perfect his new and eternal life was to be? I like to think he may well have done.

And the surprise is not that we die – that is a given for all of us. The real surprise is that we have lived at all. Christians believe that we have been given life as a gift. That's a pretty easy thing to embrace during the good times. It is less easy to embrace life as a gift during the messy, difficult times. However, given that we did not create ourselves, this life must be a gift nonetheless.

As we face mortality and come close to our own death, we are invited to think that the life we have lived has never been our own. It has always been the grace of the one who gifted it to us in order to create our being. It was a gift to us for whatever time we have been given. The giver who gifted life to us and created us, loves us so much that it is the giver's deep desire to see us return to the giver.

St Ignatius knew who the giver was. He declared it as he stepped through the doorway from this life to the next. Who is the giver? 'Oh, my God!'

God will be with us in our life and in our death. Not only that, but God will be with us after our death. In all of this we are invited to hear the gentle whisper of that most common phrase of Jesus, 'Be not afraid'.

Meditation

Spend a moment contemplating the following – if you are reading this or listening to it being read, you have life within you.

Now call to mind something that you are thankful for in the life you live and the life you have lived. Savour this for as long as you want, giving all the thanks to God. You might want to return to this or another point of gratitude once or twice a day.

Now, speak to God about how much you appreciate or have appreciated the gift of life. Acknowledge also those times you did not make the most of that gift as an opportunity to be the presence of love, joy and mercy in the world. Don't get caught up in this. Acknowledge that which needs to be acknowledged, ask for forgiveness (those who wish may seek the Sacrament of Reconciliation if it is within your religious tradition) and be aware of God's mercy and God's great love for you.

Return now to meditating on something that you are grateful for. Spend as long on this as you want.

Scripture

Psalm 23:4 Even though I walk through the darkest valley, I will fear no evil, for you are with me; your rod and your staff, they comfort me.

1 Corinthians 15:51–52 Listen, I tell you a mystery: We will not all sleep, but we will all be changed – in a flash, in the twinkling of an eye, at the last trumpet. For the trumpet will sound, the dead will be raised imperishable, and we will be changed.

John 11:25–26 Jesus said, 'I am the resurrection and the life. The one who believes in me will live, even though they die; and whoever lives by believing in me will never die.'

Action

Choose a photograph of yourself that reminds you of good times. Hold it in your hand lightly. Feel its presence in the palm of your hand.

After a moment set the photograph down (in your sacred space if you have one). Say out loud, 'Be not afraid'.

Spiritual Spring Clean

At the start of an academic year recently a friend was working through the mess that was her room. Covered in dust after some interior construction, it took some time to shape everything up, separate the rubbish from the things worth keeping, put aside clothes and stuff for recycling (the 'not used in one year' rule) and trim down to the basics. It was a whole day's work but well worth it for the energy and enthusiasm of a new start. She was commenting how much it helped her emotionally and spiritually to clear some space, get rid of old things that are no longer needed and to be open to something new. She said it was a prayer for her, a kind of retreat into the past, in order to go forward.

Of course, the practical stuff is easy to sort out, but the spiritual, the deepest part of us, is much more tricky. An essential part is a re-commitment to prayer and reflection, but what is not immediately obvious is enlisting God's help with those trickier messes: resentment, anger against another, wounds of grief or betrayal. This is what St Ignatius Loyola recommends: pray with the difficulties and 'the mess' in order that we may be free from unnecessary weights and travel light. Paradoxically it is about trying to understand it from God's point of view and God's desire to heal us, not just our point of view. This change of focus helps to break old ways of thinking and praying and move into some new beginnings, the real fresh start we long for.

Meditation

- ❋ Go to a quiet place (chapel, bedroom, park) and ask yourself how you are inside, the feelings and moods.

- ❋ Ask God to help you with the things that bother you, be aware of how much God wants to set you free.

- ❋ Specifically ask for the grace or transformation you want, if it be God's will.

- ❋ See yourself presenting these difficult things to God, like a pilgrim presenting a burden at the altar. Make it real in your imagination.

- ❋ Pray with the difficult feelings, stay with it as long as you can, and don't expect immediate results or spectacular signs (trust the slow process of the Spirit's workings).

- ❋ Use this music as background: 'The Deer's Cry'.

Scripture

Isaiah 43:18–19 'Forget the former things; do not dwell on the past. See, I am doing a new thing! Now it springs up; do you not perceive it? I am making a way in the wilderness and streams in the wasteland.'

2 Corinthians 5:17 'Therefore, if anyone is in Christ, the new creation has come: The old has gone, the new is here!'

Ezekiel 11:19 'I will give them an undivided heart and put a new spirit in them; I will remove from them their heart of stone and give them a heart of flesh.'

Action

Do a little ritual to mirror your inner process: for example, cleaning your room is a good way to represent a new start. For more difficult issues it can take a bit more thought to find an object that has some meaning for you – you could bury some stones in a field to represent hardness of heart, give away something you have held on to for years, go to a specific place that holds memories and say goodbye in your own way. Make it real.

All Will be Well

There can be so much chaos in our world and in our lives. So many people are flooded by experiences of violence, war, famine and disaster. Of course, sometimes it's not big headline news that creates chaos for us and leaves us feeling flooded. Sometimes it's everyday stuff: debt, worry, grief, poor self-image, hatred, broken relationships, addiction. At some stage or other in our lives we have all had the feeling of being flooded, of being overwhelmed.

In Psalm 29:10 we read, 'The Lord sits enthroned above the flood'. This line can remind us also of the image from Genesis of the Spirit 'hovering over the chaos'. However, God doesn't just hover above the chaos. God joins us in our chaos. It's more challenging to see God in our chaos than in the good times, but God is no less present in our chaos. God's presence consoles us and challenges us at the same time. God consoles us through God's immense love for us and assurance that all will be well in the end. God challenges us to see God in all things. When we do see God in all things, in all people, we want to reach out and help/serve those we can, thereby becoming the presence of good, i.e. God, in the chaos for others.

In this way others' worries are sorted. Others' lonely troubles are shared and halved. Others in far-off lands being bombed nightly feel the love and support of aid. Politicians make wise decisions based on respecting all life. The suicidal man walking alone along a busy road feels someone cares when the car stops and someone speaks to him. The grieving daughter knows that her daddy is at rest and looks down on her with love and pride. The man with cancer finds peace and meaning even in the face of disease.

God is hovering over the chaos. God is enthroned above the flood. Whatever flood you are experiencing, may God's presence in your flood be known to you through the love and good works of others. And may we find the opportunities to be God's presence in this world and bring the floods, the chaos to an end where we can.

Meditation

Find a quiet place to sit or lie down. Close your eyes and breathe slow, deep breaths for a minute or two. Take a moment to acknowledge the areas in your life that feel chaotic or overwhelming for you. Don't get caught up in them, rather simply acknowledge them.

Now imagine that God's love for you is like a great river of living water. In your mind's eye begin to see that river. See its wonderful colour and see its immense power. Now imagine the river meeting the bank. See yourself standing on the bank and feel the river meet your feet and legs. The water is calming and warm. As it touches your feet and legs, feel God's great love for you. Rest in the living waters of God's love for as long as you want to.

Psalm 29:10–11 The Lord sits enthroned over the flood; the Lord is enthroned as King forever. The Lord gives strength to his people; the Lord blesses his people with peace.

Genesis 8:1–3 God sent a wind over the earth, and the waters receded. Now the springs of the deep and the floodgates of the heavens had been closed, and the rain had stopped falling from the sky.

John 7:37–39 On the last day, the climax of the festival, Jesus stood and shouted to the crowds, 'Anyone who is thirsty may come to me! Anyone who believes in me may come and drink!'

Action

Fill a sink with water. For a moment look at the water and declare that it represents areas in your life where you feel flooded or overwhelmed. After a few seconds, take the plug out of the sink and see the water drain away. Declare that this is how God will work to drain the flooded areas of your life with God's great love. Watch until all the water has gone and know that all will be well.

Conclusion

CONVERSATION WITH GOD
Answered Prayer

Me: Hello ... God?

God: Hello, my friend.

Me: Thank you. You know, for that thing today.

God: Yes, I heard you call. And I answered. I always do.

Me: I really needed that to work out. So thank you.

God: You called in a new way today, my friend.

Me: Yes. I realised today that I haven't really allowed myself to truly ask for your help in my life. You know that I always bring other people before you and I truly mean it when I pray for them. But when it comes to me, I don't know, it's hard to explain.

God: You don't always fully trust me, do you?

Me: ... no, I don't always. I'm so sorry.

God: I forgive you. And I know that all people have moments of doubt. But tell me more about yours.

Me: I suppose when I feel the need to ask you for something or to ask you to be with me in something, I'm always limiting what you might do. I say, 'Please God, help me with this or that'. But in my mind I'm already telling myself not to expect you to do anything. I don't know why that is. But it is the way I have been.

God: I know. You worry that I won't come through for you. You worry that you're not asking for the right things. You worry ... a lot, don't you?

Me: I do.

God: My friend, my little one, there are things much bigger than you in my plan. I ask you to trust me. That is all. I know it is a difficult one, but I keep sending you people to tell you this. I even sent my Son. Not only did he tell you, he showed you the way. And yet ...

Me: And yet, I doubt at times. And yet, I don't fully trust you.

God: I know. I forgive you. You don't need to beat yourself up. You need to trust. Like today.

Me: Today?

God: Well when you asked for my help today, I sensed you asked in a different way. Tell me.

Me: Today I allowed myself to feel truly helpless. I allowed myself to give up on any thought of me solving my own difficulty. And I asked for you from the bottom of my heart. In my distress I cried out to you.

God: And your cry came before my ears. And I answered you; today as every other day. Even in your moments of doubt and half-hearted prayers I answer you. But remember it's not a code for immediate answers, my friend. My answers will not always be your answers. Your faith in those moments is truly wonderful to me.

Trust. And keep talking.

Me: I will ... try.

It's good to talk.

The book ends but the conversation with God is always only beginning. God is there waiting for us – in all of the messiness we experience. And as we have seen in these pages, life is by its nature messy. This is something we all find out as we journey through life. Notwithstanding the responsibility we all bear to live as well as we can within the situations we find ourselves, there is nothing we can do to prevent life becoming messy at times. That is just how it is.

In the face of great pain or sorrow it is common to want it to go away and to think that by projecting that pain, that mess, either outward or further inward, we can push it away. However, it is not possible to will ourselves out of the mess; it doesn't work and it will not do anyone any good at all. In fact, the answer does not lie in projecting the mess outward or in punishing the mess inside. The answer always lies in finding God in the mess with us; in taking our feelings to God and praying with our feelings – not against them.

We often find, with the wonderful gift of hindsight, that what appeared as disastrous in our lives was also a kind of doorway that we went through and in going through it, we learned a lot about ourselves, about the world and about the loving nature of God. This is not to minimise or take away from the hurt that the mess of life often brings. On the contrary, it is simply to acknowledge that in going deep into the mess we find ourselves in, what we also find waiting there for us, is God. God waiting to lead us out of the mess and on to better things.

A while back we met a man who was not at all religious. However, upon hearing about what we both did with our lives he confided in us that he did indeed go to church; usually at times when there was no service on and no one else in the church. When we asked him why he did this, he replied, 'It is in those moments of quietness in the church that I feel calm. I feel that everything will be ok.' How wonderful! He had found a space to be with God and in that space he found consolation.

Why not take a few moments now and reflect back on what really drew you to this book. Was there a particular mess you were/are experiencing? Were you looking for some consolation for yourself or for another? Perhaps you were just curious. Whatever your reason, spend a few moments now reflecting on what space you have found here that draws you into closer conversation, closer relationship with God. If you have found some of that space, we are very grateful to God for that and we would invite you to allow yourself to feel grateful for it as well. St Ignatius of Loyola was convinced of the importance of gratitude. He told us that it was a prerequisite for finding out what God's plan is for us. So it is good to challenge ourselves to find something to be grateful for each day – even in the mess.

And so, as you come to the end of this book, it is our hope that it will have been an experience of finding God in the mess of everyday life; even, or maybe especially, in those moments of deep hurt or deep worry. Praying our way through the book will enable us all to build up a full larder of prayer-food for the journey. Some will have chosen reading as their preferred nourishment. Other will have taken to meditation or scripture. Others again will have ritualised their prayer through action and in so doing will have built up a sacred space full of wonderful bits and pieces – themselves an image of the messiness of life!

Whatever way or ways you have prayed with this book, you have spent time deep in the mess with our loving God. And that is always a good thing.